Diego Fandango

by Lynne Rickards

illustrated by Alan Rogers

 CAMBRIDGE
UNIVERSITY PRESS

 UCL
Institute of Education

T0373851

Diego Fandango liked playing the banjo.

He wanted to play in a band.

'Who will be in my band?' said Diego.

Hippo liked playing the piano.
'Good,' said Diego.
'You can be in my band.'

Lemur liked playing the drums.

'I like drums,' said Diego.

'You can be in my band.'

Lion liked playing the trumpet.

'Good,' said Diego.

'You can be in my band, too.'

'Let's put on a show!' said Diego.

Everyone got ready.

'I will go here,' said Hippo.

'My drums will go here,' said Lemur.

'Where will I go?' said Lion.

'A-one, and a-two, and a –' shouted Diego.

The band began to play.

All the animals clapped and sang.

But then ...

'Oh, no!' said Diego.

'Look out!' shouted Hippo.

'Here comes the rain.'

Then the sun came out again.

It made a big rainbow in the sky.

'Good,' said Diego.

'Now we can put on the show!'

'Hooray,' said everyone.

Diego Fandango · Lynne Rickards

Teaching notes written by Sue Bodman and Glen Franklin

Using this book

Developing reading comprehension

In this humorous and colourfully illustrated text, Diego the Flamingo wants to play in a band, and looks for fellow musicians to play with him. A problem and resolution work to provide a simple story structure and time sequence.

Grammar and sentence structure

- Some repetition of phrase patterns, but with more variation of sentence structure evident.
- Punctuation, including the use of exclamation marks and speech marks, supports phrased and fluent reading.
- Familiar oral language structures combined with some literary language.

Word meaning and spelling

- Opportunity to rehearse a wide range of known high frequency words.
- Practice and consolidation of reading regular decodable words.
- Use of 'shouted' and 'said' to report speech.

Curriculum links

Music – Each animal played a different instrument. Listen to a piece of music to identify each instrument. What instrument is playing? Compare different instruments.

Religious studies – Linked to festivals and celebrations: why might people put on a show?

Learning Outcomes

Children can:

- read aloud using the context, sentence structure and sight vocabulary to read with expression and for meaning
- attempt new words in more challenging texts using their phonic knowledge
- comment on the events and characters in the story, making imaginative links to their own experience.

A guided reading lesson

Book Introduction

Give each child a book and read the title to them. Explain that Diego Fandango is a flamingo and draw attention to his specific features in the illustration.

Orientation

Give a brief overview of the book, using the verb in the same form as it is in text.

Diego Fandango liked playing the bango. He wants to play in a band but he has no-one to play with. So he goes out to find some other musicians who want to play with him. Let's see who he finds first.

Ask the children to turn to the title page and read the title 'Diego Fandango' running their finger under the word 'Fandango' and drawing attention to the phonemes.

Preparation

Page 4: Tell the children: *First, Diego Fandango goes to Hippo. Point to the word 'Hippo'. Good. What is Hippo playing. Yes, a piano. Point to the word 'piano'. What do you notice about Hippo and piano. That's right, they both end in 'o'.* Ask the children to read the first sentence together: *'Hippo liked playing the piano.' Do you think Hippo can be in Diego's band? Yes, I think so, too.*

Carry on through the book checking that children know and can locate the animal names and the instruments